Musical Instruments

Denise Ryan

Contents

What are different
musical instruments called?
Let's find out.

Piano

The piano is an instrument that has a keyboard. Felt hammers hit steel strings to make sounds.

A piano's keyboard has **88** keys —**52** are white and **36** are black.

grand piano

keyboard

Accordion

The accordion has a keyboard, buttons, and bellows. Players squeeze the bellows to push air through the accordion.

keyboard

The accordion is sometimes called a squeezebox.

buttons

bellows

French Horn

The French horn is a brass instrument. It has four valves and a lot of shiny, curled piping.

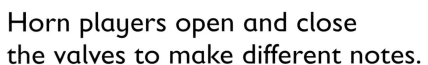

Horn players open and close the valves to make different notes.

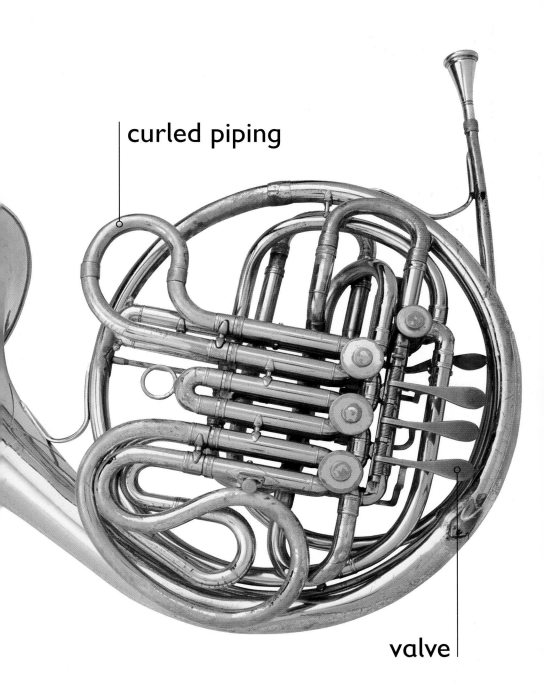

curled piping

valve

key

There are seven different kinds of saxophones.

Saxophone

A saxophone is made of brass. The player blows into the saxophone and presses the keys.

Bagpipe

Three pipes stick out of an airbag. A bagpiper blows through another pipe to fill the bag with air.

Bands of bagpipers used to lead Scottish soldiers into battle.

pipe

airbag

Electric Guitar

Electric guitars need electricity
to make loud sounds.
This guitar is made of wood.

string

wooden body

Guitarists pluck single notes or strum the strings with their fingers.

Violin

A violin has four strings and is played with a bow. The violinist draws the bow across the strings.

The string of a violin bow is made of horsehair.

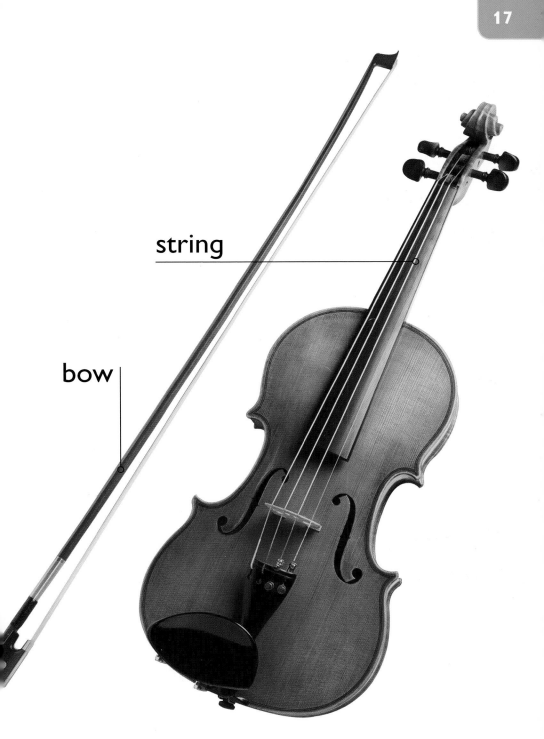

string

bow

Harp

The long strings of a harp make low notes. The harp's short strings make high notes.

A harpist plucks the harp strings with the fingers of each hand.

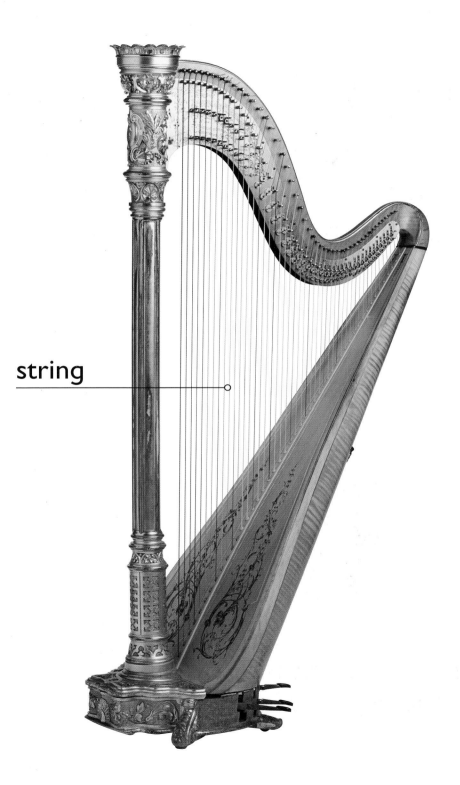

string

Drum Kit

A drum kit is a collection of drums and cymbals of different sizes.

A drummer hits the drums and cymbals with sticks or brushes.

cymbal

drum

Conga Drums

Conga drums are from Cuba.
They have tight leather tops
and wooden bodies.

You play conga drums with both hands
or with your fingers.

leather top

wooden body

Quiz

Can you match each musical instrument with its name?

conga drums   piano

harp   French horn